Constitution of the state of Michigan : as adopted in convention ... the 11th day of May, A.D. 1835.

Michigan.Michigan. Constitutional Convention

CONSTITUTION

OF THE

STATE OF MICHIGAN,

AS ADOPTED

IN CONVENTION,

BEGUN AND HELD AT THE CAPITOL, IN THE CITY OF DETROIT,

ON MONDAY, THE 11TH DAY OF MAY, A. D. 1835.

PRINTED BY ORDER OF THE CONVENTION

DETROIT.
PRINTED BY SHELDON M'KNIGHT

1835.

CONSTITUTION
OF THE
STATE OF MICHIGAN.

In Convention, begun at the city of Detroit, on the second Monday of May, in the year one thousand eight hundred and thirty five

We, the people of the Territory of Michigan, as established by the act of Congress of the eleventh of January eighteen hundred and five, in conformity to the fifth article of the ordinance providing for the government of the territory of the United States north west of the river Ohio, believing that the time has arrived when our present political condition ought to cease, and the right of self government be asserted, and availing ourselves of that provision of the aforesaid ordinance of the Congress of the United States of the thirteenth day of July, seventeen hundred and eighty seven, and the acts of Congress passed in accordance therewith, which entitled us to admission into the Union, upon a condition which has been fulfilled, do, by our delegates in convention assembled, mutually agree to form ourselves into a free and independent state, by the style and title of "The State of Michigan," and do ordain and establish the following constitution for the government of the same:

ARTICLE I.

1. All political power is inherent in the people

2. Government is instituted for the protection, security, and benefit of the people, and they have the right at all times to alter or reform the same, and to abolish one form of government and establish another, whenever the public good requires it

3. No man or set of men are entitled to exclusive or separate privileges

4. Every person has a right to worship Almighty God according to the dictates of his own conscience, and no person can of right be compelled to attend, erect, or support, against his will, any place of religious worship, or pay any tythes, taxes, or other rates for the support of any minister of the gospel or teacher of religion

5. No money shall be drawn from the treasury for the benefit of religious societies, or theological or religious seminaries

6. The civil and political rights, privileges, and capacities of no individual shall be diminished or enlarged on account of his opinions or belief concerning matters of religion

7 Every person may freely speak, write and publish his sentiments on all subjects, being responsible for the abuse of that right, and no laws shall be passed to restrain or abridge the liberty of speech or of the press In all prosecutions or indictments for libels, the truth may be given in evidence to the jury, and if it shall appear to the jury, that the matter charged as libellous is true, and was published with good motives and for justifiable ends, the party shall be acquitted and the jury shall have the right to determine the law and the fact

8 The person, houses, papers and possessions of every individual, shall be secure from unreasonable searches and seizures, and no warrant to search any place, or to seize any person or things, shall issue without describing them, nor without probable cause, supported by oath or affirmation

9 The right of trial by jury shall remain inviolate

10 In all criminal prosecutions, the accused shall have the right to a speedy and public trial by an impartial jury of the vicinage, to be confronted with the witnesses against him, to have compulsory process for obtaining witnesses in his favor, to have the assistance of counsel for his defence, and in all civil cases, in which personal liberty may be involved, the trial by jury shall not be refused

11. No person shall be held to answer for a criminal offence, unless on the presentment or indictment of a grand jury, except in cases of impeachment, or in cases cognizable by justices of the peace, or arising in the army or militia when in actual service in time of war or public danger

12. No person for the same offence shall be twice put in jeopardy of punishment, all persons shall, before conviction, be bailable by sufficient sureties, except for capital offences, when the proof is evident or the presumption great, and the privilege of the writ of habeas corpus shall not be suspended, unless when, in case of rebellion or invasion, the public safety may require it

13 Every person has a right to bear arms for the defence of himself and the state.

14 The military shall, in all cases and at all times, be in strict subordination to the civil power

15. No soldier shall, in time of peace, be quartered in any house without the consent of the owner, nor in time of war, but in a manner prescribed by law

16 Treason against the state shall consist only in levying war against it, or in adhering to its enemies, giving them aid and comfort, no person shall be convicted of treason, unless on the testimony of two witnesses to the same overt act, or on confession in open court

17 No bill of attainder, expost facto law, or law impairing the obligation of contracts, shall be passed.

18 Excessive bail shall not be required, excessive fines shall not be imposed, and cruel and unjust punishments shall not be inflicted

19 The property of no person shall be taken for public use, without just compenstion therefor

20. The people shall have the right freely to assemble together, to consult for the common good, to instruct their representatives, and to petition the legislature for redress of grievances.

21. All acts of the legislature, contrary to this or any other article of this constitution, shall be void.

ARTICLE II.

ELECTORS

1. In all elections, every white male citizen above the age of twenty one years, having resided in the state six months next preceding any election, shall be entitled to vote at such election, and every white male inhabitant of the age aforesaid, who may be a resident of this state at the time of the signing of this constitution, shall have the right of voting as aforesaid; but no such citizen or inhabitant shall be entitled to vote except in the district, county, or township, in which he shall actually reside at the time of such election.

2. All votes shall be given by ballot, except for such township officers as may, by law, be directed to be otherwise chosen.

3. Electors shall, in all cases, except treason, felony, or breach of the peace, be privileged from arrest during their attendance at elections, and in going to and returning from the same.

4. No elector shall be obliged to do militia duty on the days of election, except in time of war or public danger.

5. No person shall be deemed to have lost his residence in this state by reason of his absence on business of the United States, or of this state.

6. No soldier, seaman, or marine, in the army or navy of the United States, shall be deemed a resident of this state in consequence of being stationed in any military or naval place within the same.

ARTICLE III.

DIVISION OF THE POWERS OF GOVERNMENT

1. The powers of the government shall be divided into three distinct departments, the legislative, the executive, and the judicial; and one department shall never exercise the powers of another, except in such cases as are expressly provided for in this constitution.

ARTICLE IV.

LEGISLATIVE DEPARTMENT

1. The legislative power shall be vested in a senate and house of representatives.

2. The number of the members of the house of representatives shall never

be less than forty eight, nor more than one hundred and the senate shall, at all times, equal in number one third of the house of representatives, as nearly as may be

3. The legislature shall provide by law for an enumeration of the inhabitants of this state in the years eighteen hundred and thirty seven, and eighteen hundred and forty five, and every ten years after the said last mentioned time, and at their first session after each enumeration so made as aforesaid, and also after each enumeration made by the authority of the United States, the legislature shall apportion anew the representatives and senators among the several counties and districts, according to the number of white inhabitants

4. The representatives shall be chosen annually on the first Monday of November, and on the following day, by the electors of the several counties or districts into which the state shall be divided for that purpose. Each organized county shall be entitled to at least one representative, but no county hereafter organized shall be entitled to a separate representative, until it shall have attained a population equal to the ratio of representation hereafter established

5. The senators shall be chosen for two years, at the same time and in the same manner as the representatives are required to be chosen. At the first session of the legislature under this constitution, they shall be divided by lot from their respective districts, as nearly as may be, into two equal classes, the seats of the senators of the first class shall be vacated at the expiration of the first year, and of the second class at the expiration of the second year, so that one half thereof, as nearly as may be, shall be chosen annually thereafter

6. The state shall be divided, at each new apportionment, into a number of not less than four, nor more than eight, senatorial districts, to be always composed of contiguous territory, so that each district shall elect an equal number of senators annually, as nearly as may be, and no county shall be divided in the formation of such districts

7. Senators and representatives shall be citizens of the United States, and be qualified electors in the respective counties and districts which they represent, and a removal from their respective counties or districts shall be deemed a vacation of their seats

8. No person holding any office under the United States, or of this state, officers of the militia, justices of the peace, associate judges of the circuit and county courts, and postmasters excepted, shall be eligible to either house of the legislature

9. Senators and representatives shall, in all cases except treason, felony, or breach of the peace, be privileged from arrest, nor shall they be subject to any civil process, during the session of the legislature, nor for fifteen days next before the commencement and after the termination of each session

10. A majority of each house shall constitute a quorum to do business, but a smaller number may adjourn from day to day, and may compel the attendance

of absent members, in such manner and under such penalties as each house may provide. Each house shall choose its own officers.

11. Each house shall determine the rules of its proceedings, and judge of the qualifications, elections, and returns of its own members, and may, with the concurrence of two-thirds of all the members elected, expel a member, but no member shall be expelled a second time for the same cause, nor for any cause known to his constituents antecedent to his election.

12. Each house shall keep a journal of its proceedings, and publish the same, except such parts as may require secrecy, and the yeas and nays of the members of either house, on any question, shall, at the request of one-fifth of the members present, be entered on the journal. Any member of either house shall have liberty to dissent from and protest against any act or resolution which he may think injurious to the public or an individual, and have the reasons of his dissent entered on the journal.

13. In all elections by either or both houses, the votes shall be given *viva voce*, and all votes on nominations made to the senate shall be taken by yeas and nays, and published with the journal of its proceedings.

14. The doors of each house shall be open, except when the public welfare shall require secrecy; neither house shall, without the consent of the other, adjourn for more than three days, nor to any other place than that where the legislature may then be in session.

15. Any bill may originate in either house of the legislature.

16. Every bill passed by the legislature shall, before it becomes a law, be presented to the governor; if he approve, he shall sign it, but if not, he shall return it, with his objections, to that house in which it originated, who shall enter the objections at large upon their journal, and proceed to reconsider it. If, after such reconsideration, two-thirds of all the members present agree to pass the bill, it shall be sent, with the objections, to the other house, by whom it shall likewise be reconsidered, and if approved also by two thirds of all the members present in that house, it shall become a law; but in such cases, the votes of both houses shall be determined by yeas and nays, and the names of the members voting for or against the bill shall be entered on the journals of each house respectively. And if any bill be not returned by the governor within ten days, Sundays excepted, after it has been presented to him, the same shall become a law, in like manner as if he had signed it, unless the legislature, by their adjournment, prevent its return, in which case it shall not become a law.

17. Every resolution to which the concurrence of the senate and house of representatives may be necessary, except in cases of adjournment, shall be presented to the governor, and, before the same shall take effect, shall be proceeded upon in the same manner as in the case of a bill.

18. The members of the legislature shall receive, for their services, a compensation to be ascertained by law, and paid out of the public treasury, but no increase of the compensation shall take effect during the term for which the

members of either house shall have been elected, and such compensation shall never exceed three dollars a day

19 No member of the legislature shall receive any civil appointment from the governor and senate, or from the legislature, during the term for which he is elected

20 The governor shall issue writs of election to fill such vacancies as may occur in the senate and house of representatives

21 The legislature shall meet on the first Monday in January in every year, and at no other period, unless otherwise directed by law, or provided for in this constitution

22 The style of the laws of this state shall be—*Be it enacted by the Senate and House of Representatives of the State of Michigan*

ARTICLE V.

EXECUTIVE DEPARTMENT

1 The supreme executive power shall be vested in a governor, who shall hold his office for two years, and a lieutenant governor shall be chosen at the same time and for the same term

2 No person shall be eligible to the office of governor or lieutenant governor, who shall not have been five years a citizen of the United States, and a resident of this state two years next preceding the election

3 The governor and lieutenant governor shall be elected by the electors at the times and places of choosing members of the legislature. The persons having the highest number of votes for governor and lieutenant governor shall be elected, but in case two or more have an equal and the highest number of votes for governor or lieutenant governor, the legislature shall by joint vote choose one of the said persons, so having an equal and the highest number of votes, for governor or lieutenant governor

4 The returns of every election for governor and lieutenant governor shall be sealed up and transmitted to the seat of government, by the returning officers, directed to the president of the senate, who shall open and publish them in the presence of the members of both houses

5 The governor shall be commander in chief of the militia, and of the army and navy of this state

6 He shall transact all executive business with the officers of government, civil and military; and may require information, in writing, from the officers in the executive department, upon any subject relating to the duties of their respective offices

7 He shall take care that the laws be faithfully executed

8 He shall have power to convene the legislature on extraordinary occasions He shall communicate by message to the legislature, at every session, the con-

dition of the state, and recommend such matters to them as he shall deem expedient

9. He shall have power to adjourn the legislature to such time as he may think proper, in case of a disagreement between the two houses with respect to the time of adjournment, but not to a period beyond the next annual meeting

10. He may direct the legislature to meet at some other place than the seat of government, if that shall become, after its adjournment, dangerous from a common enemy or a contagious disease.

11. He shall have power to grant reprieves and pardons after conviction, except in cases of impeachment.

12. When any office, the appointment to which is vested in the governor and senate, or in the legislature, becomes vacant during the recess of the legislature, the governor shall have power to fill such vacancy by granting a commission, which shall expire at the end of the succeeding session of the legislature

13. In case of the impeachment of the governor, his removal from office, death, resignation, or absence from the state, the powers and duties of the office shall devolve upon the lieutenant governor until such disability shall cease, or the vacancy be filled

14. If, during the vacancy of the office of governor, the lieutenant governor shall be impeached, displaced, resign, die or be absent from the state, the president of the senate, pro tempore, shall act as governor, until the vacancy be filled

15. The lieutenant governor shall, by virtue of his office, be president of the senate, in committee of the whole, he may debate on all questions, and, when there is an equal division, he shall give the casting vote

16. No member of congress, nor any other person, holding office under the United States, or this state, shall execute the office of governor

17. Whenever the office of governor or lieutenant governor becomes vacant, the person exercising the powers of governor for the time being shall give notice thereof, and the electors shall, at the next succeeding annual election for members of the legislature, choose a person to fill such vacancy

18. The governor shall, at stated times, receive for his services a compensation, which shall neither be increased nor diminished during the term for which he has been elected

19. The lieutenant governor, except when acting as governor, and the president of the senate, pro tempore, shall each receive the same compensation as hall be allowed to the speaker of the house of representatives.

20. A great seal for the state shall be provided by the governor, which shall contain the device and inscriptions represented and described in the papers relating thereto, signed by the president of the convention, and deposited in the office of the secretary of the territory It shall be kept by the secretary of state, and all official acts of the governor, his approbation of the laws excepted, shall be thereby authenticated.

B

21. All grants and commissions shall be in thioname, and by the authority, of the people of the state of Michigan

ARTICLE VI.

JUDICIAL DEPARTMENT

1. The judicial power shall be vested in one supreme court, and in such other courts as the legislature may from time to time establish

2. The judges of the supreme court shall hold their offices for the term of seven years, they shall be nominated, and by and with the advice and consent of the senate, appointed by the governor   They shall receive an adequate compensation, which shall not be diminished during their continuance in office.— But they shall receive no fees nor perquisites of office, nor hold any other office of profit or trust under the authority of this state, or of the United States

3. A court of probate shall be established in each of the organized counties

4. Judges of all county courts, associate judges of circuit courts, and judges of probate shall be elected by the qualified electors of the county in which they reside, and shall hold their offices for four years

5. The supreme court shall appoint their clerk or clerks, and the electors of each county shall elect a clerk, to be denominated a county clerk, who shall hold his office for the term of two years, and shall perform the duties of clerk to all the courts of record to be held in each county, except the supreme court and court of probate.

6. Each township may elect four justices of the peace, who shall hold their offices for four years, and whose powers and duties shall be defined and regulated by law. At their first election they shall be classed and divided by lot into numbers one, two, three, and four, to be determined in such manner as shall be prescribed by law, so that one justice shall be annually elected in each township thereafter   A removal of any justice from the township in which he was elected, shall vacate his office.   In all incorporated towns, or cities, it shall be competent for the legislature to increase the number of justices

7. The style of all process shall be "*In the name of the people of the state of Michigan;*" and all indictments shall conclude against the peace and dignity of the same

ARTICLE VII.

CERTAIN STATE AND COUNTY OFFICERS.

1. There shall be a secretary of state, who shall hold his office for two years, and who shall be appointed by the governor, by and with the advice and consent of the senate   He shall keep a fair record of the official acts of the legislative and executive departments of the government, and shall, when required, lay the same, and all matters relative thereto, before either branch of

the legislature, and shall perform such other duties as shall be assigned him by law.

2. A state treasurer shall be appointed by a joint vote of the two houses of the legislature, and shall hold his office for the term of two years.

3. There shall be an auditor general and an attorney general for the state, and a prosecuting attorney for each of the respective counties, who shall hold their offices for two years, and who shall be appointed by the governor, by and with the advice and consent of the senate, and whose powers and duties shall be prescribed by law

4. There shall be a sheriff, a county treasurer, and one or more coroners, a register of deeds, and a county surveyor, chosen by the electors in each of the several counties once in every two years, and as often as vacancies shall happen. The sheriff shall hold no other office, and shall not be capable of holding the office of sheriff longer than four in any term of six years, he may be required by law to renew his security from time to time, and in default of giving such security, his office shall be deemed vacant, but the county shall never be made responsible for the acts of the sheriff.

ARTICLE VIII.

IMPEACHMENTS AND REMOVALS FROM OFFICE.

1. The house of representatives shall have the sole power of impeaching all civil officers of the state for corrupt conduct in office, or for crimes and misdemeanors, but a majority of all the members elected shall be necessary to direct an impeachment

2. All impeachments shall be tried by the senate When the governor or lieutenant governor shall be tried, the chief justice of the supreme court shall preside Before the trial of an impeachment, the members of the court shall take an oath or affirmation truly and impartially to try and determine the charge in question according to the evidence, and no person shall be convicted without the concurrence of two thirds of the members present Judgment, in cases of impeachment, shall not extend further than to removal from office, but the party convicted shall be liable to indictment and punishment according to law

3. For any reasonable cause, which shall not be sufficient ground for the impeachment of the judges of any of the courts, the governor shall remove any of them on the address of two thirds of each branch of the legislature, but the cause or causes for which such removal may be required, shall be stated at length in the address

4. The legislature shall provide by law for the removal of justices of the peace, and other county and township officers, in such manner and for such cause as to them shall seem just and proper

ARTICLE IX.

MILITIA

1 The legislature shall provide by law for organizing and disciplining the militia, in such manner as they shall deem expedient, not incompatible with the constitution and laws of the United States.

2 The legislature shall provide for the efficient discipline of the officers, commissioned and non commissioned, and musicians, and may provide by law for the organization and discipline of volunteer companies

3. Officers of the militia shall be elected or appointed in such manner as the legislature shall from time to time direct, and shall be commissioned by the governor

4. The governor shall have power to call forth the militia, to execute the laws of the state, to suppress insurrections, and repel invasions

ARTICLE X.

EDUCATION

1 The governor shall nominate, and by and with the advice and consent of the legislature in joint vote, shall appoint a superintendent of public instruction, who shall hold his office for two years, and whose duties shall be prescribed by law

2 The legislature shall encourage, by all suitable means, the promotion of intellectual, scientifical, and agricultural improvement. The proceeds of all lands that have been or hereafter may be granted by the United States to this state, for the support of schools, which shall hereafter be sold or disposed of, shall be and remain a perpetual fund, the interest of which, together with the rents of all such unsold lands, shall be inviolably appropriated to the support of schools throughout the state.

3. The legislature shall provide for a system of common schools, by which a school shall be kept up and supported in each school district, at least three months in every year; and any school district neglecting to keep up and support such a school, may be deprived of its equal proportion of the interest of the public fund.

4. As soon as the circumstances of the state will permit, the legislature shall provide for the establishment of libraries, one at least in each township, and the money which shall be paid by persons as an equivalent for exemption from military duty, and the clear proceeds of all fines assessed in the several counties for any breach of the penal laws, shall be exclusively applied to the support of said libraries

5 The legislature shall take measures for the protection, improvement, or other disposition of such lands as have been or may hereafter be reserved or granted by the United States to this state for the support of a University, and

the funds accruing from the rents or sale of such lands, or from any other source for the purpose aforesaid, shall be and remain a permanent fund for the support of said University, with such branches as the public convenience may hereafter demand for the promotion of literature, the arts and sciences, and as may be authorized by the terms of such grant. And it shall be the duty of the legislature, as soon as may be, to provide effectual means for the improvement and permanent security of the funds of said University.

ARTICLE XI.

PROHIBITION OF SLAVERY.

1. Neither slavery nor involuntary servitude shall ever be introduced into this state, except for the punishment of crimes of which the party shall have been duly convicted.

ARTICLE XII.

MISCELLANEOUS PROVISIONS

1. Members of the legislature, and all officers, executive and judicial, except such inferior officers as may by law be exempted, shall, before they enter on the duties of their respective offices, take and subscribe the following oath or affirmation "I do solemnly swear, or affirm, (as the case may be,) that I will support the constitution of the United States, and the constitution of this state, and that I will faithfully discharge the duties of the office of   according to the best of my ability." And no other oath, declaration, or test, shall be required as a qualification for any office or public trust.

2. The legislature shall pass no act of incorporation, unless with the assent of at least two thirds of each house.

3. Internal improvement shall be encouraged by the government of this state; and it shall be the duty of the legislature, as soon as may be, to make provision by law for ascertaining the proper objects of improvement in relation to roads, canals, and navigable waters; and it shall also be their duty to provide by law for an equal, systematic, and economical application of the funds which may be appropriated to these objects.

4. No money shall be drawn from the treasury but in consequence of appropriations made by law; and an accurate statement of the receipts and expenditures of the public money shall be attached to and published with the laws annually.

5. Divorces shall not be granted by the legislature, but the legislature may by law authorize the higher courts to grant them, under such restrictions as they may deem expedient.

6 No lottery shall be authorized by this state, nor shall the sale of lottery tickets be allowed

7 No county now organized by law shall ever be reduced, by the organization of new counties, to less than four hundred square miles

8 The governor, secretary of state, treasurer, and auditor general, shall keep their offices at the seat of government

9 The seat of government for this state shall be at Detroit, or at such other place or places as may be prescribed by law, until the year eighteen hundred and forty-seven, when it shall be permanently located by the legislature

10 The first governor and lieutenant governor shall hold their offices until the first Monday of January eighteen hundred and thirty eight, and until others shall be elected and qualified, and thereafter, they shall hold their offices for two years, and until their successors shall be elected and qualified

11 When a vacancy shall happen, occasioned by the death, resignation, or removal from office of any person holding office under this state, the successor thereto shall hold his office for the period which his predecessor had to serve, and no longer, unless again chosen or reappointed

ARTICLE XIII.

MODE OF AMENDING AND REVISING THE CONSTITUTION

1. Any amendment or amendments to this constitution may be proposed in the senate or house of representatives, and if the same shall be agreed to by a majority of the members elected to each of the two houses, such proposed amendment or amendments shall be entered on their journals, with the yeas and nays taken thereon, and referred to the legislature then next to be chosen, and shall be published for three months previous to the time of making such choice And if in the legislature next chosen as aforesaid, such proposed amendment or amendments shall be agreed to by two-thirds of all the members elected to each house, then it shall be the duty of the legislature to submit such proposed amendment or amendments to the people, in such manner and at such time as the legislature shall prescribe, and if the people shall approve and ratify such amendment or amendments, by a majority of the electors qualified to vote for members of the legislature, voting thereon, such amendment or amendments shall become part of the constitution

2. And if at any time two-thirds of the senate and house of representatives shall think it necessary to revise or change this entire constitution, they shall recommend to the electors, at the next election for members of the legislature, to vote for or against a convention and if it shall appear that a majority of the electors voting at such election have voted in favor of calling a convention, the legislature shall at its next session provide by law for calling a convention to be holden within six months after the passage of such law, and such convention shall consist of a number of members not less than that of both branches of the legislature

SCHEDULE.

1 That no inconvenience may arise from a change of the territorial government to a permanent state government, it is declared that all writs, actions, prosecutions, contracts, claims, and rights, of individuals and of bodies corporate, shall continue as if no change had taken place in this government, and all process which may, before the organization of the judicial department under this constitution, be issued under the authority of the territory of Michigan, shall be as valid as if issued in the name of the state.

2 All laws now in force in the territory of Michigan, which are not repugnant to this constitution, shall remain in force until they expire by their own limitations, or be altered or repealed by the legislature

3 All fines, penalties, forfeitures, and escheats, accruing to the territory of Michigan, shall accrue to the use of the state

4 All recognizances heretofore taken, or which may be taken before the organization of the judicial department under this constitution, shall remain valid, and shall pass over to, and may be prosecuted in the name of, the state. And all bonds executed to the governor of this territory, or to any other officer in his official capacity, shall pass over to the governor or other proper state authority, and to their successors in office, for the uses therein respectively expressed, and may be sued for and recovered accordingly All criminal prosecutions and penal actions, which have arisen, or which may arise before the organization of the judicial department under this constitution, and which shall then be depending, may be prosecuted to judgment and execution in the name of the state

5. All officers, civil and military, now holding their offices and appointments in this territory under the authority of the United States, or under the authority of this territory, shall continue to hold and exercise their respective offices and appointments until superseded under this constitution

6 The first election for governor, lieutenant governor, members of the state legislature, and a representative in the congress of the United States, shall be held on the first Monday in October next, and on the succeeding day And the president of the convention shall issue writs to the sheriffs of the several counties or districts, or, in case of vacancy, to the coroners, requiring them to cause such election to be held on the days aforesaid, in their respective counties or districts The election shall be conducted in the manner prescribed, and by the township officers designated as inspectors of elections, and the returns made as required, by the existing laws of the territory, or by this constitution. *Provided, however,* that the returns of the several townships in the district composed of the unorganized counties of Ottawa, Ionia, Kent, and Clinton, shall be

made to the clerk of the township of Kent in said district, and the said township clerk shall perform the same duties, as, by the existing laws of the territory, devolve upon the clerks of the several counties in similar cases

7. The first meeting of the legislature shall be at the city of Detroit, on the first Monday in November next, with power to adjourn to any other place.

8 All county and township officers shall continue to hold their respective offices, unless removed by the competent authority, until the legislature shall, in conformity to the provisions of this constitution, provide for the holding of elections to fill such offices respectively.

9. This constitution shall be submitted, at the election to be held on the first Monday in October next, and on the succeeding day, for ratification or rejection, to the electors qualified by this constitution to vote at all elections, and if the same be ratified by the said electors, the same shall become the constitution of the state of Michigan. At the election aforesaid, on such of the ballots as are for the said constitution, shall be written or printed the word "yes," and on those which are against the ratification of said constitution, the word "no" And the returns of the votes on the question of ratification or rejection of said constitution, shall be made to the president of this convention at any time before the first Monday in November next, and a digest of the same communicated by him to the senate and house of representatives on that day.

10. And if this constitution shall be ratified by the people of Michigan, the president of this convention shall, immediately after the same shall be ascertained, cause a fair copy thereof, together with an authenticated copy of the act of the legislative council, entitled "An act to enable the people of Michigan to form a constitution and state government," approved January 26, 1835, providing for the calling of this convention, and also a copy of so much of the last census of this territory as exhibits the number of the free inhabitants of that part thereof which is comprised within the limits in said constitution defined as the boundaries of the proposed state of Michigan, to be forwarded to the President of the United States, together with an expression of the decided opinion of this convention, that the number of the free inhabitants of said proposed state now exceeds the number requisite to constitute two congressional districts, and the respectful request of this convention, in behalf of the people of Michigan, that all said matters may be by him laid before the congress of the United States at their next session

11. In case of the failure of the president of this convention to perform the duties prescribed by this constitution, by reason of his absence, death, or from any other cause, said duties shall be performed by the secretaries of this convention

12 Until the first enumeration shall be made as directed by this constitution the county of Wayne shall be entitled to eight representatives, the county of Monroe to four representatives, the county of Washtenaw to seven representatives, the county of St Clair to one representative, the county of St. Joseph to two representatives, the county of Berrien to one representative, the

county of Calhoun to one representative, the county of Jackson to one representative, the county of Cass to two representatives, the county of Oakland to six representatives, the county of Macomb to three representatives; the county of Lenawee to four representatives, the county of Kalamazoo, and the unorganized counties of Allegan and Barry, to two representatives, the county of Branch to one representative, the county of Hillsdale to one representative, the county of Lapeer to one representative, the county of Saginaw, and the unorganized counties of Genesee and Shiawasse, to one representative, the county of Michilimackinac to one representative, the county of Chippewa to one representative, and the unorganized counties of Ottawa, Kent, Ionia, and Clinton, to one representative.

And for the election of Senators the state shall be divided into five districts, and the apportionment shall be as follows The county of Wayne shall compose the first district, and elect three senators, the counties of Monroe and Lenawee shall compose the second district, and elect three senators, the counties of Hillsdale, Branch, St Joseph, Cass, Berrien, Kalamazoo, and Calhoun, shall compose the third district, and elect three senators, the counties of Washtenaw and Jackson shall compose the fourth district, and elect three senators; and the counties of Oakland, Lapeer, Saginaw, Macomb, St Clair, Michilimackinac and Chippewa, shall compose the fifth district, and elect four senators.

Any country attached to any county for judicial purposes, if not otherwise represented, shall be considered as forming part of such county, so far as regards elections for the purpose of representation in the legislature.

JOHN BIDDLE, *President.*

JOHN NORVELL,	ORIN HOWE,
JOHN M'DONELL,	EMANUEL CASE,
JNO. R. WILLIAMS,	E. MUNDY,
ALPHEUS WHITE,	ORRIN WHITE,
AMOS STEVENS,	ISAAC VOORHEIS,
CONRAD TEN EYCK,	RANDOLPH MANNING,
LEWIS BEAUFAIT,	SENECA NEWBERRY,
PETER VAN EVERY,	JOSHUA B TAYLOR.
J D. DAVIS,	ELIJAH COOK,
CALEB HERRINGTON,	EBENEZERE RAYNAL,
AMMON BROWN,	JOHN ELLENWOOD,
THEOPH'S E TALLMAN,	JEREMIAH RIGGS,
GEO. W. FERRINGTON,	BENJAMIN B MORRIS,
ASA H. OTIS,	WILLIAM PATRICK,

CH. F. IRWIN,
WM. WOODBRIDGE,
EDWARD D. ELLIS,
JAMES J. GODFROY,
PETER P. FERRY,
ROBERT McCLELLAND,
DAVID WHITE,
ELIPHALET CLARK,
SAMUEL INGERSOLL,
LEMUEL COLBATH,
J. V. D. SUTPHEN,
ROSS WILKINS,
SELLECK C. BOUGHTON,
ALLEN HUTCHINS,
JOHN J. ADAM,
JOSEPH HOWELL, Jr.
JOSEPH H. PATTERSON,
DARIUS COMSTOCK,
ALEXANDER R. TIFFANY
GILBERT SHATTUCK,
ABEL GODARD,
WILLIAM MOORE,
ROBERT PURDY,
JOHN BREWER,
ALPHEUS COLLINS,
M. P. STUBBS,
RICHARD BROWER,
RUFUS CROSSMAN,
NATHANIEL NOBLE,
RUSSELL BRIGGS,
JONATHAN CHASE,
SAMUEL WHITE,
THOMAS CURTIS,
NORMAN DAVISON,
SAMUEL AXFORD,
EPHRAIM CALKIN,
JACOB TUCKER,
JOHN S AXFORD,
HENRY PORTER,
SOLOMON PORTER,
JOHN CLARKE,
RALPH WADHAMS,
TOWNSEND E. GIDLEY,
ROSWELL B REXFORD,
LEWIS T. MILLER,
ISAAC E. CRARY,
EZRA CONVIS,
LUCIUS LYON,
WILLIAM H. WELCH,
HEZEKIAH G. WELLS,
JAMES NEWTON,
JAMES ODELL,
BALDWIN JENKINS,
JOHN S BARRY,
HUBBEL LOOMIS,
MARTIN G SHELLHOUSE
TITUS B WILLARD,
ELIJAH LACY
MICHAEL DOUSMAN,
BELA CHAPMAN.

ORDINANCE.

Be it ordained by the convention assembled to form a constitution for the state of Michigan, in behalf, and by authority of the people of said state, that the following propositions be submitted to the Congress of the United States, which, if assented to by that body, shall be obligatory on this state.

1st. Section numbered sixteen in every surveyed township of the public lands, and where such section has been sold or otherwise disposed of, other lands equivalent thereto, and as contiguous as may be, shall be granted to the state for the use of schools.

2d. The seventy two sections of land set apart and reserved for the use and support of a university, by an act of Congress approved on the twentieth day of May, eighteen hundred and twenty six, entitled "An act concerning a seminary of learning in the territory of Michigan," shall, together with such further quantities as may be agreed upon by Congress, be conveyed to the State, and shall be appropriated solely to the use and support of such university, in such manner as the legislature may prescribe.

3d. Four entire sections of land, to be selected under the direction of the legislature, from any of the unappropriated lands belonging to the United States shall be granted to the state for its use in establishing a seat of government.

4th. Seven hundred sections of the unappropriated public lands lying within this state, shall be designated, under the direction of the legislature, and granted to the state for the purposes of internal improvement. Said lands, or the proceeds of the sale thereof, shall be appropriated to aid the state in constructing one or more rail roads or canals across the peninsula, from Lake Erie or Detroit River to Lake Michigan, and also to aid in the construction of such other roads and canals, and in the improvement of such rivers, as the legislature may designate. And five per cent of the nett proceeds of the sale of all lands lying within the territory or state, which shall be sold by Congress from and after the first day of January, eighteen hundred and thirty-six, after deducting all expenses incident to the same, shall also be appropriated, two fifths thereof for the purposes before described in this proposition, and three-fifths for the encouragement of learning.

5th. All salt springs within the state, and the lands reserved for the use of the same, at least one section including each spring, shall be granted to the state, to be used or disposed of as the legislature may direct.

6th. The roads commenced in this state, for the construction of which appropriations have been made by Congress, shall be completed and put in repair at the expense of the United States

7th The first senators and representative or representatives elected to Congress from this state, are hereby authorized and empowered to make or assent to such other propositions, or to such variations of the propositions herein made, as the interests of the state may require, and any such changes or new propositions, when approved by the legislature, shall be as obligatory as if the assent of his convention were given thereto, and all stipulations entered into by the legislature in pursuance of the authority herein conferred, shall be considered articles of compact between the United States and this state; and the legislature is hereby further authorized to declare, in behalf of the people of Michigan, if such declaration be proposed by Congress, that they will never interfere with the primary disposal, under the authority of the United States, of the vacant lands within the limits of this state

JOHN BIDDLE, President.

CHARLES W WHIPPLE, } Secretaries
MARSHAL J BACON,

CPSIA information can be obtained
at www.ICGtesting.com
Printed in the USA
LVHW060930250122
709154LV00024B/1077